LOUISA MAY ALCOTT

~ *Her Girlhood Diary* ~

LOUISA MAY ALCOTT

✦ *Her Girlhood Diary* ✦

*Edited, compiled, and with an
introduction and narrative by*
CARY RYAN

Illustrated by
MARK GRAHAM

Troll Medallion

Permissions appear on page 42.
Compilation, narrative text, and introduction
copyright © 1993 by Cary Ryan.
Illustrations copyright © 1993 by Mark Graham.
Published by Troll Associates, Inc. All rights reserved.
No part of this book may be used or reproduced in any manner
whatsoever without written permission from the publisher.
First published in hardcover by BridgeWater Books.
Printed in the United States of America.
10   9   8   7   6   5   4   3   2

Library of Congress Cataloging-in-Publication Data
Alcott, Louisa May, 1832-1888
Louisa May Alcott : her girlhood diary / compiled and edited by Cary Ryan ;
illustrations by Mark Graham.
p.   cm.
Includes bibliographical references.
Summary: Excerpts from the author's diaries, letters,
and early poetic efforts, written between the ages of ten and
fourteen, reveal her thoughts and feelings.
ISBN 0-8167-3139-X (lib.) — ISBN 0-8167-3150-0 (pbk.)
1. Alcott, Louisa May, 1832-1888 — Biography — Youth — Juvenile literature.
2. Alcott, Louisa May, 1832-1888 — Diaries — Juvenile literature. 3. Authors,
American — 19th century — Diaries — Juvenile literature. [1. Alcott, Louisa May,
1832-1888. 2. Authors, American. 3. Diaries.] I. Ryan, Cary. II. Graham, Mark,
1952- ill. III. Title.
PS1018.A427 1993 818'.403 — dc20 93-22343 [B]

*To my mother, who was my help and comfort,
and to my father — that rarest of events,
a great teacher — who truly saw and "unfolded"
what lay in my child's nature.*

~& ACKNOWLEDGMENTS &~

I am most grateful to the Pratt family for their permission to reprint material from the Houghton Library at Harvard University; to Cynthia Barton, the author of a biography-in-progress of Abigail May Alcott, for her generous help; to Maggie Stier, Curator of the Fruitlands Museums, and Bob Farwell, Director of the Fruitlands Museums, for their invaluable aid and for permission to reprint material from the manuscript in the Fruitlands Museums; to Leslie Morris, Curator of Manuscripts, for permission to reprint material from the manuscripts in the Houghton Library, Harvard University, and Vicki Denby and Betty Falsey of the Houghton Library for their kind assistance; to Amy Saulich, of Little, Brown and Company, for her knowledgeable advice and for permission to reprint material from *The Journals of Louisa May Alcott*; and to the most helpful of the many sources I've consulted, Ednah D. Cheney's *Louisa May Alcott: Her Life, Letters, and Journals*; *The Journals of Louisa May Alcott*, edited by Joel Myerson, Daniel Shealy, and Madeleine B. Stern; and Madelon Bedell's *The Alcotts: Biography of a Family*.

I owe a special debt of gratitude to my editor, Joanne Mattern, and to the book's designer, Leslie Bauman — the lights at the end of the tunnel; to Olga Litowinski, for her support along the way; and to John Kavanaugh, who has a way with darkness. I am more grateful than I can say to

Louisa May Alcott

Mark Howson and to Michael and Daphne Grosset Ryan for their unerring judgment and unfaltering belief in the words; and to my mother, Catharine McMillan Clauser, for her astute, sensitive, and loving guidance.

To Lawrence Marek, without whose steadfast love there would be no book, I owe a debt that is unrepayable.

Editor's Note

Little of Louisa May Alcott's girlhood diary has survived—much of it destroyed by Louisa herself before her death. The diary entries, letters, and poems in this book have been printed exactly as they have come down to us, spelling errors, stylistic inconsistencies, and oddities of punctuation intact. The quotations from *Little Women* have been reprinted exactly as they appear in the 1915 Little, Brown edition, which most faithfully reproduces Louisa's own text.

So as to avoid confusion, I have referred to Louisa's mother by her signature name, Abby Alcott, and to Louisa's youngest sister as Abby May Alcott, even though they shared the middle name May (along with the nickname Abba).

CONTENTS

Introduction

"Wouldn't it be fun if all the castles in the air which we make could come true, and we could live in them?" asks *Little Women*'s Jo March.

"You'd have nothing but horses, inkstands, and novels in yours," says her sister Meg.

"Would n't I, though? I'd have a stable full of Arabian steeds, rooms piled with books, and I'd write of a magic inkstand, so that my works should be ... famous.... I want to do something splendid before I go into my castle, — something heroic or wonderful, that won't be forgotten after I'm dead. I don't know what, but I'm on the watch for it, and mean to astonish you all, some day. I think I shall write books, and get rich and famous: that would suit me, so that is *my* favorite dream."

And that is just what Louisa May Alcott did when she

wrote *Little Women,* the heroic, wonderful story of her own girlhood. Since *Little Women* was published more than a hundred years ago, generations of readers have found faithful, lifelong friends in its heroines: beautiful, kind Meg (in real life Louisa's older sister, Anna); shy, sensitive Beth (Louisa's younger sister and special pet, Lizzie); charming, sometimes infuriating Amy (the "baby" of the Alcott family, Abby May); and high-spirited, loyal Jo — who was Louisa herself.

Meg, Beth, Amy, and Jo draw us into their charmed world today as irresistibly as ever. It is a safe world, not because it is free of hardship or sorrow, but because nothing can defeat the March sisters so long as they stay true to each other — and true to themselves. Their strength lies in their loyalty, and in their knowledge that, no matter what life puts in their path, it cannot prevent them from being who they choose to be.

Little Women's readers have long wished they could know the girl whose life was the key to this strength. Now they can. Here, published for the first time for young readers, are entries from the girlhood diary Louisa May Alcott began when she was ten years old.

Louisa's diary might have been Jo's own. It is a window on the real-world poverty and spiritual richness that Louisa celebrated — and lamented — in *Little Women.* But it is more. It is the diary of "a struggling human girl, like hundreds of others," as Louisa would call Jo. In it Louisa writes of her love for her sisters (and sometimes her fury at them) and talks of the ideas, lessons, and books that inspired (and bored) her. She confides her innermost thoughts, struggles with the overpowering emotions and unruly moods that constantly undid her, and records her uphill battle to "manage" herself.

"I don't *talk* about myself ;" Louisa said, "yet must always think of the wilful, moody girl I try to manage, and in my journal I write of her to see how she gets on." Now we can watch her getting on — transforming herself from a troubled ten-year-old into the young woman who would create the first liberated girl in American literature.

Louisa May Alcott was born on November 29, 1832, in Germantown, Pennsylvania. She was the second daughter of Abigail ("Abby") May Alcott and the philosopher Amos Bronson Alcott. Nineteenth century New England was not ready for some of Bronson Alcott's ideas about education. When he introduced sex education — and a black student — into his Temple School in Boston, angry parents forced him to shut the school down. Undiscouraged, he moved his family to Concord, Massachusetts, to start again.

In the barn behind their Concord cottage (described as Meg's first home in *Little Women*), the Alcott girls put on the plays they loved so much. Here, Louisa wrote, they "dramatized the fairy tales in great style. Our giant came tumbling off a loft when Jack cut down the squash-vine running up a ladder to represent the immortal bean. Cinderella rolled away in a vast pumpkin, and a long black pudding was lowered by invisible hands to fasten itself on the nose of the woman who wasted her three wishes."

In the garden the girls staged pageants of their favorite

book, *The Pilgrim's Progress,* and picked fresh strawberries for Henry David Thoreau, Ralph Waldo Emerson, Nathaniel Hawthorne, and the other philosophers and writers who were friends of the Alcott family.

Like Emerson and Thoreau, Bronson Alcott belonged to a group of idealistic thinkers called the New England Transcendentalists. The Transcendentalists were leaders in the fight for women's rights and the abolition of slavery. They believed that the good in human nature could be realized through self-reliance, self-discipline, and self-sacrifice. In 1843, just two months before Louisa began her diary, Bronson Alcott and his friend Charles Lane decided to put these beliefs into practice. In nearby Harvard they began an experimental farm, called Fruitlands. Here people could come to live and work, in hopes of providing for themselves and helping those who had less than they.

In her diary Louisa writes of the simple, hard life at Fruitlands, where she and her sisters rose early to take cold showers before their morning lessons with Charles Lane, did their tasks, and sewed doll's dresses to sell to neighboring children. They ate no meat and wore rough linen clothing because they believed it was wrong to take the life of a fellow creature, or even its coat (wool), or to use a product of slavery (cotton). Their spare life brought home the lesson they had been taught from birth: However little they had, they must give a share of it to those who had less. And because their idealist father proved to be a poor real-world provider, what they had was often very little indeed.

When Louisa realized how poor her family was — and saw the suffering it caused her beloved mother — she decided to devote her life to the task of supporting her family. At the age of seventeen she became a schoolteacher. The following year she worked for seven weeks as a servant — digging paths through snow, carrying well water, and splitting firewood — all to earn four dollars. She continued to slave for the next twenty years as a housemaid, teacher, and seamstress to keep her family from poverty. "Every day is a battle," she wrote, "and I'm so tired I don't want to live ; only it's cowardly to die till you have done something."

Though Louisa sacrificed her life for those she loved, she never betrayed her creative self — the part of her that burned to do something splendid. Instead, she drew upon her gift to realize her life's dream of caring for her family and becoming "perfectly independent."

The fairy tales, suspense tales, romances, and war stories she wrote in her teens sold for very little. But *Hospital Sketches*, a book of letters she had written home as a Civil War nurse, won her acclaim. "Fifteen years of hard grubbing may be coming to something after all," she wrote, "& I may yet 'pay all the debts, fix the house, send [Abby] May to Italy & keep the old folks cosy,' as I've said I would so long yet so hopelessly." And in 1868 *Little Women* brought her fame beyond anything she had dreamed of — and freed her family from poverty forever.

Louisa's writing has shown generations of readers who they are gently alongside what they could become, reassuring them that the distance in between is only a human step. We can now watch Louisa herself take that step in her earliest writings of all.

CHAPTER ONE

Uphill Battles

Jo . . . had hard times trying to curb the fiery spirit which was continually getting her into trouble ; her anger never lasted long, and, having humbly confessed her fault, she sincerely repented, and tried to do better. . . . but her bosom enemy was always ready to flame up and defeat her ; and it took years of patient effort to subdue it.

Little Women

Louisa May Alcott was born with "the wild exuberance of a powerful nature" — "fit for the scuffle of things," her father complained. Louisa was the one who ran away from home, who would do anything on a dare (even when the boys wouldn't), who almost drowned in the frog pond. "I always thought I must have been a deer or a horse in some former state, because it was such a joy to run," she wrote. "No boy could be my friend till I had beaten him in a race, and no girl if she refused to climb trees, leap fences, and be a tomboy."

In other words, Louisa was the opposite of everything her family — and nineteenth century New England — required a young woman to be. She was not proper, or obedient, or meek. She was, instead, her own person. Or, as she was taught to see it, willful, selfish, and proud.

In her diary Louisa writes of her battles against her "wilful," "proud" self and her "dreadful" temper, and her despair when she loses these battles. But winning or losing her battles, Louisa remains true to her rebellious "tomboy" core. And her diary sings with joy when she rescues herself from despair through poetry — at first the poetry of others, and then poetry of her own.

Poetry also made the failure of Fruitlands bearable to Louisa. At ten, when she began her diary, she did not yet understand how poor her own family was — and thought only of helping the "truly" poor. Soon enough, though, she realized that the Fruitlands community could not support itself — let alone take care of others.

. . . .

Ten Years Old.

September 1st. [1843] — I rose at five and had my bath. I love cold water! Then we had our singing-lesson with Mr. Lane. After breakfast I washed dishes, and ran on the hill till nine, and had some thoughts, — it was so beautiful up there. Did my lessons, — wrote and spelt and did sums ; and Mr. Lane read a story, "The Judicious Father": How a rich girl told a poor girl not to look over the fence at the flowers, and was cross to her because she was unhappy. The father heard her do it, and made the girls change clothes. The poor one was glad to do it, and he told her to keep them. But the rich one was very sad ; for she had to wear the old ones a week, and after that she was good to shabby girls. I liked it very much, and I shall be kind to poor people.

Father asked us what was God's noblest work. Anna said *men,* but I said *babies.* Men are often bad ; babies never are. We had a long talk, and I felt better after it, and *cleared up.*

We had bread and fruit for dinner. I read and walked and played till supper-time. We sung in the evening. As I went to bed the moon came up very brightly and looked at me. I felt sad because I have been cross to-day, and did not mind Mother. I cried, and then I felt better, and said that piece from [the singer] Mrs. [Lydia] Sigourney, "I must not tease my mother." I get to sleep saying poetry, — I know a great deal.

Thursday, 11th. — [The anti-slavery reformer] Mr. Parker Pillsbury came, and we talked about the poor slaves. I had a music lesson with Miss P[age]. I hate her, she is so fussy. I ran in the wind and played be a horse, and had a lovely time in the woods with Anna and Lizzie. We were fairies, and made gowns and paper wings. I "flied" the highest of all. . . .

It rained when I went to bed, and made a pretty noise on the roof.

Sunday, 21st. — Father and Mr. Lane have gone to N[ew] H[ampshire] to preach. It was very lovely. . . . Anna and I got supper. In the eve I read [Oliver Goldsmith's] "[The] Vicar of Wakefield." I was cross to-day, and I cried when I went to bed. I made good resolutions, and felt better in my heart. If I only *kept* all I make, I should be the best girl in the world. But I don't, and so am very bad.

Louisa and her mother read and wrote in each other's diaries, and continually exchanged letters and poems. Louisa wrote this letter to her mother on October 8, Abby Alcott's birthday:

To Abigail May Alcott

Fruitlands
Sunday

Dearest Mother

I have spent a very pleasant morning and I hardly dare to speak to Annie [Anna] for fear she should speak unkindly and get me angry. O she is so very very cross I cannot love her[,] it seems as though she did every thing to trouble me but I will try to love her better, I hope you have spent a pleasant morning. Please axcept[sic] this book mark from your affectionate daughter.

LOUISA

It is not very pretty but it is all I have to give.

LOUY

Eleven years old. *Thursday, [November] 29th.* — It

4

was Father's and my birthday. We had some nice presents. We played in the snow before school. Mother read [Maria Edgeworth's] "Rosamond" when we sewed. Father asked us in the eve what fault troubled us most. I said my bad temper.

Wednesday. [December] — ... I wrote in my Imagination Book, and enjoyed it very much. Life is pleasanter than it used to be, and I don't care about dying any more. Had a splendid run, and got a box of cones to burn. Sat and heard the pines sing a long time. Read Miss Fredrika Bremer's "[The] Home" in the eve. Had good dreams, and woke now and then to think, and watch the moon. I had a pleasant time with my mind, for it was happy.

January, 1845, Friday. — Did my lessons, and in the P.M. mother read [Sir Walter Scott's] "Kenilworth" to us while we sewed. It is splendid! I got angry and called Anna mean. Father told me to look out the word in the Dic., and it meant "base," "contemptible." I was so ashamed to have called my dear sister that, and I cried over my bad tongue and temper.

We have had a lovely day. All the trees were covered with ice, and it shone like diamonds or fairy palaces. I made a piece of poetry about winter: —

The stormy winter's come at last,
  With snow and rain and bitter blast ;

Ponds and brooks are frozen o'er,
    We cannot sail there any more.

The little birds are flown away
    To warmer climes than ours ;
They'll come no more till gentle May
    Calls them back with flowers.

Oh, then the darling birds will sing
    From their neat nests in the trees.
All creatures wake to welcome Spring,
    And flowers dance in the breeze.

With patience wait till winter is o'er,
    And all lovely things return ;
Of every season try the more
    Some knowledge or virtue to learn.

Wednesday. — I am so cross I wish I had never been born.

Tuesday. — More people coming to live with us ; I wish we could be together, and no one else. I don't see who is to clothe and feed us all, when we are so poor now. I was very dismal, and then went to walk and made a poem.

DESPONDENCY

Silent and sad,
When all are glad,
And the earth is dressed in flowers ;
When the gay birds sing

Till the forests ring,
As they rest in woodland bowers.

Oh, why these tears,
And these idle fears
For what may come to-morrow ?
The birds find food
From God so good,
And the flowers know no sorrow.

If He clothes these
And the leafy trees,
Will He not cherish thee ?
Why doubt His care ;
It is everywhere,
Though the way we may not see.

Then why be sad
When all are glad,
And the world is full of flowers ?
With the gay birds sing,
Make life all Spring,
And smile through the darkest hours.

"I used to imagine my mind a room in confusion, and I was to put it in order ; so I swept out useless thoughts and dusted foolish fancies away, and furnished it with good resolutions and began again," Louisa later wrote. And even when she was a girl, she ordered her mind by writing. "But," she added, "cobwebs get in. I'm not a good house-keeper, and never get my room in nice order. I once wrote a poem about it when I was fourteen, and called it 'My Little Kingdom.' It is still hard to rule it, and always will be I think."

MY LITTLE KINGDOM.

A LITTLE kingdom I possess,
    Where thoughts and feelings dwell,
And very hard I find the task
    Of governing it well ;
For passion tempts and troubles me,
    A wayward will misleads,
And selfishness its shadow casts
    On all my words and deeds.

How can I learn to rule myself,
    To be the child I should,
Honest and brave, nor ever tire
    Of trying to be good ?
How can I keep a sunny soul
    To shine along life's way ?
How can I tune my little heart
    To sweetly sing all day ?

Dear Father, help me with the love
    That casteth out my fear ;
Teach me to lean on thee, and feel
    That thou art very near,
That no temptation is unseen,
    No childish grief too small,
Since thou, with patience infinite,
    Doth soothe and comfort all.

Uphill Battles

I do not ask for any crown
    But that which all may win,
Nor seek to conquer any world
    Except the one within.
Be thou my guide until I find,
    Led by a tender hand,
Thy happy kingdom in *myself*,
    And dare to take command.

❧ CHAPTER TWO ❧

Lessons

"If [Demi] is old enough to ask the questions he is old enough to receive true answers. I am not putting the thoughts into his head, but helping him unfold those already there. These children are wiser than we are, and I have no doubt the boy understands every word I have said to him."

Mr. March, of his grandson, Little Women

Bronson Alcott believed that a child's "divine nature" could be "awakened" by dialogues between teacher and pupil — question-and-answer conversations that "unfolded" what was already within the child. As Louisa wrote, "My father taught in the wise way which unfolds what lies in the child's nature, as a flower blooms, rather than crammed it, like a Strassburg goose, with more than it could digest." But to us today Bronson's dialogues with his daughters (and his students) might seem more like bullying sessions that led his pupils to accept the "divine nature" within Bronson himself. In fact, he directed much of his daughters' education toward destroying their very sense of self — a barrier, he felt, to unity with the divine, especially as it had chosen to express itself in him.

So, if Louisa was at war with herself, that war had its

roots in her father's teachings. She surely believed she must do battle against the "proud," "wilful," "selfish" side of her nature because her father had decided, when she was still an infant, that her "noble" nature needed "taming down to docility."

Still, there was a playful, and even tender side to Bronson's relationship with his daughters. He cared for them when they were quite young, allowing them to romp to their hearts' content. Like Mr. March in *Little Women,* he taught them the alphabet by lying on the floor with his long legs up in the air so they could "write" with these "pencils." And he held bedtime conversations with them "about the state of [their] little consciences and the conduct of [their] childish lives which," Louisa wrote, "never [would] be forgotten."

Bronson Alcott encouraged imagination in his daughters. He nightly told or read them stories and praised them when they made up their own. And though there may have been gaps in Louisa's education — she "dodged" arithmetic and grammar whenever she could — he nurtured in her what she needed to become a writer: a love and mastery of language and a freedom and power of expression. And he urged her to write letters, poems, the plays that were such an important part of the Alcott girls' lives, and the diary you are reading now.

Louisa's diary makes it clear that her education would have been a lot happier had Bronson's partner Charles Lane not become the girls' tutor at Fruitlands (something Louisa never liked to remember). Mr. Lane may have been a respected scholar, but Louisa and her sisters did not like him or his lessons. It was probably a touch of rebellion that prompted Louisa to name "love of cats" in her diary when "Mr. L." asked her to list the "vices" she wished "less of." Cats were a particular passion of the Alcott girls, who wrote plays starring their own beloved pets and organized elaborate funerals for them when these cherished creatures devastated them by dying.

. . . .

Friday, Nov. 2nd. [1843] — Anna and I did the work. In the evening Mr. Lane asked us, "What is man ?" These were our answers : A human be-ing ; an animal with a mind ; a creature ; a body ; a soul and a mind. After a long talk we went to bed very tired.

[January 1845] —

A Sample of our Lessons.

"What virtues do you wish more of ?" asks Mr. L[ane]. I answer : —

Patience,	Love,	Silence,
Obedience,	Generosity,	Perseverance,
Industry,	Respect,	Self-denial.

"What vices less of ?"

Idleness,	Wilfulness,	Vanity,
Impatience,	Impudence,	Pride,
Selfishness,	Activity,	Love of cats.

Mr. L.   L.

How can you get what you need ? By trying.

How do you try ? By resolution and perseverance.

How gain love ? By gentleness.

What is gentleness ? Kindness, patience, and care for other people's feelings.

Who has it ? Father and Anna.

Who means to have it ? Louisa, if she can.

["She never got it," Louisa added years later.]

No. 3.

What are the most valuable kinds of self-denial ? Appetite, temper.

How is self-denial of temper known ? If I control my temper, I am respectful and gentle, and every one sees it.

What is the result of this self-denial ? Every one loves me, and I am happy.

Why use self-denial ? For the good of myself and others.

How shall we learn this self-denial ? By resolving, and then trying *hard*.

What then do you mean to do ? To resolve and try.

Louisa found a better teacher than Mr. Lane in nature. Henry David Thoreau was her guide to the woods, and her "wise mother, anxious to give [her] a strong body

to support a lively brain, turned [her] loose in the country
and let [her] run wild, learning of Nature what no books
can teach."

Thursday. — Read [Sir Walter Scott's] "Heart of
Mid-Lothian," and had a very happy day. Miss
Ford [who helped care for the girls] gave us a bot-
any lesson in the woods. I am always good there.
In the evening Miss Ford told us about the bones
in our bodies, and how they get out of order. I
must be careful of mine, I climb and jump and run
so much.

Friday. — I read "Philothea," by [the Alcotts'
friend] Mrs. [Lydia Maria] Child. I found this
that I liked in it. [The Greek philosopher] Plato
said: —

"[']When I hear a note of music I can at once
strike its chord. Even as surely is there everlasting
harmony between the soul of man and the invisible forms of creation.['] If there were no innocent
hearts there would be no white lilies. . . . I often
think flowers are the angel's alphabet whereby
they write on hills and fields mysterious and beautiful lessons for us to feel and learn."

CHAPTER THREE

A Helping Hand

They always looked back before turning the corner, for their mother was always at the window, to nod and smile, and wave her hand to them. Somehow it seemed as if they couldn't have gone through the day without that ; for, whatever their mood might be, the last glimpse of that motherly face was sure to affect them like sunshine.

Little Women

Abby Alcott, the model for *Little Women*'s Marmee, was Louisa's truest source of strength and comfort. It was she who helped Louisa bridge the distance between who she was and who she was becoming.

Abby knew what it would cost her unruly daughter to bend to the world's expectations, having done it herself. But she also knew how unhappy Louisa would be if she could not learn what came so hard to her: patience in waiting for what she wanted, and acceptance when she could not have it.

In the letters and poems she wrote to Louisa and the messages she left in Louisa's diary, Abby counsels her gently, echoing Marmee's advice to Meg, Beth, Amy, and

Jo: "When you feel discontented, think over your blessings, and be grateful. . . . try to deserve them, lest they should be taken away entirely, instead of increased."

Abby was certain that Louisa was destined to be a great writer. She encouraged her daughter's gifts and "great yearning nature" in every way she could. In return she won Louisa's undying devotion.

. . . .

A letter to Louisa from her mother, 1842

COTTAGE IN CONCORD.

DEAR DAUGHTER, — Your tenth birthday has arrived. May it be a happy one, and on each returning birthday may you feel new strength and resolution to be gentle with sisters, obedient to parents, loving to every one, and happy in yourself.

I give you the pencil-case I promised, for I have observed that you are fond of writing, and wish to encourage the habit.

Go on trying, dear, and each day it will be easier to be and do good. You must help yourself, for the cause of your little troubles is in yourself ; and patience and courage only will make you what mother prays to see you, — her good and happy girl.

October 8th. [1843] — When I woke up, the first thought I got was, "It's Mother's birthday : I must be very good." I ran and wished her a happy birthday, and gave her my kiss. After breakfast we gave her our presents. I had a moss cross and a piece of poetry for her.

We did not have any school, and played in the woods and got red leaves. In the evening we danced and sung, and I read a story about "Contentment." I wish I was rich, I was good, and we were all a happy family this day.

Thursday, [November] 29th. — . . . I told mother I liked to have her write in my book. She said she would put in more, and she wrote this to help me: —

DEAR LOUY, — Your handwriting improves very fast. Take pains and do not be in a hurry. I like to have you make observations about our conversations and your own thoughts. It helps you to express them and to understand your little self. Remember, dear girl, that a diary should be an epitome of your life. May it be a record of pure thought and good actions, then you will indeed be the precious child of your loving mother.

Saturday 23 [December] — In the morning mother went to the Village and I had my lessons and then helped Annie get dinner after which mother came home and Annie went [on] an errand for mother to Mr Lovejoys

we stayed a little while to see their little baby

boy   I often wish I had a little brother but as I have not I shall try to be contented with what I have got, (for Mother often says if we are not contented with what we have got it will be taken away from us) and I think it is very true. When we returned from Mr. Lovejoys, we played till supper time   in the evening we played cards and when I went to bed I felt happy for I had been obedient and kind to Father and Mother and gentle to my sisters, I wish I could be gentle always.

A letter to Louisa from her mother

CONCORD, 1843.

DEAR LOUY, — I enclose a picture for you which I always liked very much, for I imagined that you might be just such an industrious daughter and I such a feeble but loving mother, looking to your labor for my daily bread.

Keep it for my sake and your own, for you and I always liked to be grouped together.

MOTHER.

The lines I wrote under the picture in my journal: —

TO MOTHER.

I hope that soon, dear mother,
    You and I may be

In the quiet room my fancy
    Has so often made for thee, —

The pleasant, sunny chamber,
    The cushioned easy-chair,
The book laid for your reading,
    The vase of flowers fair ;

The desk beside the window
    Where the sun shines warm and bright :
And there in ease and quiet
    The promised book you write ;

While I sit close beside you,
    Content at last to see
That you can rest, dear mother,
    And I can cherish thee.

[Louisa later added: "The dream came true, and for the last ten years of her life Marmee sat in peace, with every wish granted, even to the 'grouping together;' for she died in my arms."]

Thursday. [January 1845] — ... I found this note from dear mother in my journal: —

MY DEAREST LOUY, — I often peep into your diary, hoping to see some record of more happy days. "Hope, and keep busy," dear daughter, and in all perplexity or trouble come freely to your

MOTHER.

DEAR MOTHER, — You *shall* see more happy days,

and I will come to you with my worries, for you
are the best woman in the world.

L. M. A.

A letter from Louisa to her mother, 1845

To Abigail May Alcott

Dearest Mother

 I have tryed to be more contented and I think
I have been more so. I have been thinking about
my little room which I suppose I never shall have.
I should want to be there about all the time and I
should go there and sing and think.

> But I'll be contented
>   With what I have got
>   Of folly repented
>   Then sweet is my lot.

from your trying daughter

LOUY

A letter to Louisa from her mother

HILLSIDE, CONCORD.

DEAR, — . . . . Patience, dear, will give us content, if nothing else. Be assured the little room you
long for will come, if it is necessary to your peace
and well-being. Till then try to be happy with the
good things you have. They are many, — more
perhaps than we deserve, after our frequent com-
plaints and discontent.

A Helping Hand

Be cheerful, my Louy, and all will be gayer
for your laugh, and all good and lovely things will
be given to you when you deserve them. . . .

MOTHER.

❧ CHAPTER FOUR ❧

Losses

*Beth was too shy to enjoy society, and Jo too
wrapped up in her to care for anyone else ; so they were
all in all to each other, and came and went, quite unconscious of . . . those about them, who watched with sympa-
thetic eyes the strong sister and the feeble one, always
together, as if they felt instinctively that a long separa-
tion was not far away.*

Little Women

Louisa's family was everything to her. Her diary re-
veals how painfully she suffered when she was parted
from them, even when the separations were short.

. . . .

Tuesday, [October] 12th. [1843] — After lessons I
ironed. We all went to the barn and husked corn.
It was good fun. We worked till eight o'clock and
had lamps. . . . Mother and Lizzie [*Little Women*'s
Beth] are going to Boston. I shall be very lonely
without dear little Betty [Lizzie], and no one will
be as good to me as mother. I read in [the Greek

25

biographer] Plutarch. I made a verse about sunset: —

Softly doth the sun descend
    To his couch behind the hill,
Then, oh, then, I love to sit
    On the mossy banks beside the rill.

Anna thought it was very fine; but I didn't like it very well.

Tuesday, [November] 20th. — I rose at five, and after breakfast washed the dishes, and then helped mother work. Miss P. is gone, and Anna in Boston with Cousin Louisa. I took care of Abby [May] in the afternoon. In the evening I made some pretty things for my dolly. Father and Mr. L. had a talk, and father asked us if *we* saw any reason for us to separate. Mother wanted to, she is so tired. I like it [Fruitlands], but not the school part or Mr. L.

For some time Charles Lane had been trying to break up the Alcotts' marriage, which he felt was a threat to the Fruitlands commune. Shortly before Louisa wrote this entry, her mother had announced that she was leaving the farm, and her husband must decide whether to come with her or stay behind with Mr. Lane. Bronson could not at first make up his mind and asked his daughters what they thought.

In the end it was Mr. Lane who left Fruitlands — a victory Louisa celebrates in her next entry. But she was also frightened and miserable, probably because she feared her father would leave them too. He had done this once before, when Louisa was two. Louisa's fears were justified, for soon afterward Bronson went to Boston — though in the end he returned to his family.

December 10th. — I did my lessons, and walked in the afternoon. Father read to us in dear Pilgrim's Progress. Mr. L. was in Boston, and we were glad. In the eve father and mother and Anna and I had a long talk. I was very unhappy, and we all cried. Anna and I cried in bed, and I prayed God to keep us all together.

Sunday 24th — After breakfast Father started for Boston[.] When he was gome [gone] I read and wrote till dinner after which I washed the dishes and then I made some presents for Christmass. . . . I did not go to bed till 10 oclock

Anna, too, probably returned to Boston to stay with the girls' cousin Louisa Willis soon after this.

Sunday. — We all went into the woods to get moss for the *arbor* Father is making for *Mr. Emerson.* I miss Anna so much. I made two verses for her: —

TO ANNA.

Sister, dear, when you are lonely,
    Longing for your distant home,
And the images of loved ones
    Warmly to your heart shall come,

Then, mid tender thoughts and fancies,
   Let one fond voice say to thee,
"Ever when your heart is heavy,
   Anna, dear, then think of me."
Think how we two have together
   Journeyed onward day by day,
Joys and sorrows ever sharing,
   While the swift years roll away.
Then may all the sunny hours
   Of our youth rise up to thee,
And when your heart is light and happy,
   Anna, dear, then think of me.

Wednesday. — ... A long letter from Anna. She sends me a picture of Jenny Lind, the great singer. She must be a happy girl. I should like to be famous as she is. Anna is very happy ; and I don't miss her as much as I shall by and by in the winter.

Perhaps these temporary separations caused Louisa such pain because she sensed that longer ones were to come. For when Louisa was twenty-five, her beloved sister Lizzie died after a long illness. Louisa, speaking as Jo, expressed her anguish when she wrote of Beth's death in *Little Women*:

> Jo felt as if a veil had fallen between her heart and Beth's ; but when she put out her hand to lift it up, there seemed something sacred in the silence, and [she] waited for Beth to speak. . . .

One day Beth told her. Jo thought she was asleep, she lay so still ; and, putting down her book, sat looking at her with wistful eyes, trying to see signs of hope in the faint color on Beth's cheeks. But she could not find enough to satisfy her, for the cheeks were very thin, and the hands seemed too feeble to hold even the rosy little shells they had been gathering. It came to her then more bitterly than ever that Beth was slowly drifting away from her, and her arms instinctively tightened their hold upon the dearest treasure she possessed. . . .

" Jo, dear, I 'm glad you know it. I 've tried to tell you, but I could n't."

There was no answer except her sister's cheek against her own, not even tears ; for when most deeply moved, Jo did not cry. . . .

" I 've known it for a good while, dear, and now I 'm used to it, it is n't hard to think of or to bear. Try to see it so, and don't be troubled about me, because it 's best ; indeed it is." . . .

" I don't care what becomes of anybody but you, Beth. You *must* get well."

" I want to, oh, so much ! I try, but every day I lose a little, and feel more sure that I shall never gain it back. It's like the tide, Jo, when it turns, it goes slowly, but it can't be stopped."

" It *shall* be stopped, your tide must not turn so soon, nineteen is too young. Beth, I can't let you go. I 'll work and pray and fight against it.

29

I 'll keep you in spite of everything ; there must be ways, it can't be too late. God won't be so cruel as to take you from me," cried poor Jo rebelliously, for her spirit was far less piously submissive than Beth's. . . .

" Jo, dear, don't hope any more ; it won't do any good, I 'm sure of that. We won't be miserable, but enjoy being together while we wait. We 'll have happy times, for I don't suffer much, and I think the tide will go out easily, if you help me."

This was Louisa's diary entry on the day of Lizzie's death:

March 14th. [1858] — My dear Beth died at three this morning, after two years of patient pain. Last week she put her work away, saying the needle was "too heavy," and having given us her few possessions, made ready for the parting in her own simple, quiet way. For two days she suffered much, begging for ether, though its effect was gone. Tuesday she lay in Father's arms, and called us round her, smiling contentedly as she said, "All here!" I think she bid us good-by then, as she held our hands and kissed us tenderly. Saturday she slept, and at midnight became unconscious, quietly breathing her life away till three; then, with one last look of the beautiful eyes, she was gone. . . .

For the last time we dressed her in her usual

cap and gown, and laid her on her bed, — at rest at last. . . .

On Monday Dr. Huntington read the Chapel service, and we sang her favorite hymn. Mr. Emerson, Henry Thoreau, . . . and John Pratt [Anna's husband-to-be], carried her out of the old home to the new one at Sleepy Hollow chosen by herself. So the first break comes, and I know what death means, — a liberator for her, a teacher for us.

There were more "breaks" to come. When Louisa's mother died in 1877, she wrote: "My only comfort is that I *could* make her last years comfortable, and lift off the burden she had carried so bravely all these years. . . . I think I shall soon follow her, and am quite ready to go now she no longer needs me." Two years later Ralph Waldo Emerson, the family's "best & tenderest friend," told Louisa that her youngest sister had died in Europe, leaving her two-month-old daughter in Louisa's care. And eight years later Louisa's father died, just two days before Louisa's own death at the age of fifty-five. Louisa had long been ill and in pain herself, but she had turned a deaf ear to the demands of her body until her duty to her family was done.

CHAPTER FIVE

A Room of Her Own

"You must take my place, Jo, and be everything to father and mother when I 'm gone. They will turn to you, don't fail them ; and if it 's hard to work alone, remember that I don't forget you, and that you 'll be happier in doing that than writing splendid books or seeing all the world ; for love is the only thing that we can carry with us when we go, and it makes the end so easy."

"I 'll try, Beth ;" and then and there Jo renounced her old ambition, pledged herself to a new and better one, acknowledging the poverty of other desires, and feeling the blessed solace of a belief in the immortality of love.

Little Women

It was in her own room, in the Concord house known as Hillside, that Louisa dedicated herself to this "new and better" life's ambition. Hillside — bought with an inheritance from Abby Alcott's father and a gift from Ralph Waldo Emerson a year after Fruitlands failed — was the model for Meg, Beth, Amy, and Jo's house in *Little Women* and the scene of the happiest days of Louisa's life. It was here that she, at last, got the room she had longed for but feared she would never have. The room was a symbol of Louisa's passage into womanhood — a fitting place in which to pledge herself to the duty she would shoulder till her death.

. . . .

Thirteen Years Old.

HILLSIDE.

March, 1846. — I have at last got the little room I have wanted so long, and am very happy about it. It does me good to be alone, and Mother has made it very pretty and neat for me. My work-basket and desk are by the window, and my closet is full of dried herbs that smell very nice. The door that opens into the garden will be very pretty in summer, and I can run off to the woods when I like.

I have made a plan for my life, as I am in my teens, and no more a child. I am old for my age, and don't care much for girl's things. People think I'm wild and queer ; but Mother understands and helps me. I have not told any one about my plan ; but I'm going to *be* good. I've made so many resolutions, and written sad notes, and cried over my sins, and it does n't seem to do any good! Now I'm going to *work really,* for I feel a true desire to improve, and be a help and comfort, not a care and sorrow, to my dear mother.

Louisa did *work really* and was never anything but a help and comfort to her mother. But that did not keep her from running wild in the woods that spoke as no human voice could to this passionate girl in whom "genius burned."

A Room of Her Own

From a letter Louisa wrote to her friend Sophia Gardner on September 23, 1845

I had a beautiful walk the other day ... to a pond called Finch pond, there we found lots of grapes and some lovely flowers ; and now, if you won't laugh, I 'll tell you something — ... all of us waded across it, a great big pond a mile long and half a mile wide, we went splashing along making the fishes run like mad before our big claws, when we got to the other side we had a funny time getting on our shoes and unmentionables, and we came tumbling home all wet and muddy ; but we were happy enough, for we came through the woods bawling and singing like crazy folks. Yesterday we went over a little way from our house into some great big fields full of apple-trees, which we climed[sic], tearing our clothes off our backs (luckily they were old) and breaking our bones, playing tag and all sorts of strange things. We are dreadfull wild people here in Concord, we do all the sinful things you can think of.

Thursday, [November] 30th. — I had an early run in the woods before the dew was off the grass. The moss was like velvet, and as I ran under the arches of yellow and red leaves I sang for joy, my heart was so bright and the world so beautiful. I stopped at the end of the walk and saw the sunshine out over the wide "Virginia meadows."

It seemed like going through a dark life or

grave into heaven beyond. A very strange and solemn feeling came over me as I stood there, with no sound but the rustle of the pines, no one near me, and the sun so glorious, as for me alone. It seemed as if I *felt* God as I never did before, and I prayed in my heart that I might keep that happy sense of nearness all my life.

And so she did, even though her struggle lasted a lifetime. But what a struggle it was. The woman who emerged from it not only carried love with her when she went but left it behind for us, in the best-loved book ever written for young women — a book that redefines what it means to be born a girl.

❧ CHRONOLOGY ❧

1831	March 16	Anna Bronson Alcott is born in Philadelphia
1832	November 29	Louisa May Alcott is born in Germantown, Pennsylvania
1834	September	The Alcotts move to Boston, where Bronson Alcott starts his Temple School
1835	June 24	Elizabeth ("Lizzie") Sewall Alcott is born in Boston
1840	July 26	Abby ("Abba") May Alcott is born in Concord, Massachusetts
1843	June 1	The Alcotts and Charles Lane move to Fruitlands in Harvard, Massachusetts
1845	January	The Alcotts move into the house known as Hillside in Concord
1858	March 14	Lizzie Alcott dies
1862	December 13	Louisa becomes a Civil War nurse
1863	August	*Hospital Sketches* is published
1868	October 1	*Little Women*, Part One, is published
1869	April 14	*Little Women*, Part Two, is published
1870	April	*An Old-Fashioned Girl* is published
1871	June	*Little Men* is published in America

1875	September 25	*Eight Cousins* is published
1876	November	*Rose in Bloom* is published
1877	November 25	Louisa's mother, Abigail Alcott, dies
1878	March 22	Abba May, now called May, is married to Ernest Nieriker
	October 15	*Under the Lilacs* is published
1879	November 8	May's daughter, Louisa May ("Lulu") Nieriker, is born in Paris
	December 29	May dies
1880	September 19	Lulu Nieriker comes to live with Louisa in Boston
	October 9	*Jack and Jill* is published
1886	October 9	*Jo's Boys* is published in America
1888	March 4	Louisa's father, Bronson Alcott, dies
	March 6	Louisa dies

❧ SOURCES ❧

The diary entries, letters, and poems in this book have been gathered together from a number of different sources. The October 8, 1843, letter on page 4 and the diary entries for December 23, 1843 (pages 19–20), and December 24, 1843 (page 27), are from the manuscript in the Fruitlands Museums in Harvard, Massachusetts. All other diary entries, the poem on pages 8–9, and the letters on pages 18, 20–21, and 22–23 are from Ednah D. Cheney's *Louisa May Alcott: Her Life, Letters, and Journals* (Boston: Roberts Brothers, 1889), pages 23, 24, 32, 35–48; 96–103; 296–301. The letter on page 35 is from Annie M. L. Clark, *The Alcotts in Harvard* (Lancaster, Mass.: J.C.L. Clark, 1902), pages 41–43.

The *Little Women* quotations on pages ix, x, 1, 11, 17, 18, 25, 28–30, and 33 are from Louisa May Alcott, *Little Women or Meg, Jo, Beth and Amy* (Boston: Little, Brown and Company, 1915), pages 151–153, 463, 78–79, 493–494, 38, 47–48, 395–396, 396–400, and 446 respectively. The quotations on pages xi, xiii, and 7–8 are from Louisa's May and August 1850 journal, as cited in Cheney, pages 59–63; the quotation on pages 30–31 is from her March 1858 journal, as cited in Cheney, pages 96–103; and the quotation on page 31 is from her December 1877 journal, as cited in Cheney, pages 299–300. The second quotation on page xiii is from Louisa's October 1863 journal, as reprinted, from the manuscript in the Houghton Library, Harvard University, in *The Journals of Louisa May Alcott*, edited by Joel Myerson, Daniel Shealy, and Madeleine B. Stern (Boston: Little, Brown and Company, 1989), page 121. The childhood recollections on pages xi, 1, 11, 12, and 14–15 are from Cheney, pages 29–31. The Bronson Alcott quotations on pages 1 and 12 are from his *Researches on Childhood*, pages 27 and 270, and his *Observations on the Spiritual Nurture of my Children*, page 136, both in the Alcott Pratt Collection of the Houghton Library.

✥ INDEX ✥

Louisa May Alcott

ABOUT THE EDITOR

A graduate of Wellesley College, **Cary Ryan** was a children's book editor before becoming a freelance editor, translator, and writer. She has collaborated on translations of books from French into English, and on books and articles in the fields of psychology, philosophy, and science.

ABOUT THE ILLUSTRATOR

Mark Graham has illustrated *Roommates, Charlie Anderson, Greenbrook Farm, Home by Five, Lottie's Dream, Shadows Are About,* and the forthcoming *Michael and the Cats.* He has exhibited his paintings in galleries across the country, and teaches painting and drawing.